Serve Up Tennis

Contents

written by Diana Fre

I0895205

Red Rocket Readers™

Engineered by Flying Start Books

skills and equipment

To learn to play tennis, you must master all the skills. You will need:

- A racket
- Tennis clothes
- Sports shoes
- A cap

Go to a tennis class to learn how to hold your racket and how to serve the ball. Start by hitting a ball on a wall. Serve lots of times so you get good at it.

Tennis can be played with 2 or 4 players.

A tennis court is marked with lines and has a net in the middle.

Important games need an umpire. They sit on a tall seat looking down on the court – to call if a ball is in or out.

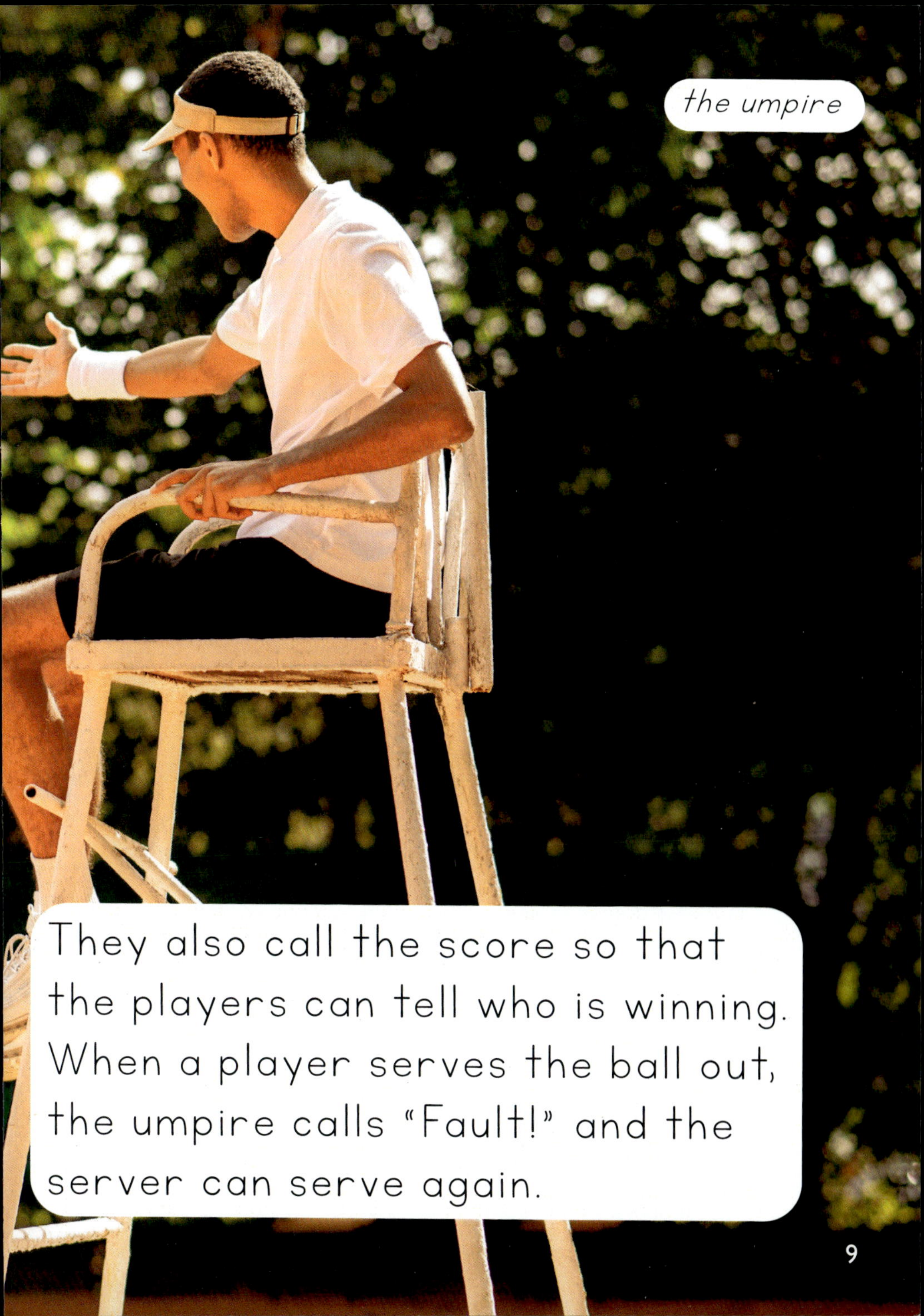

They also call the score so that the players can tell who is winning. When a player serves the ball out, the umpire calls "Fault!" and the server can serve again.

When a ball is hit from player to player its called a rally - which is also the way to start a game. The winner of a rally is the player who serves first.

rally-up

Go to see strong players playing. You can learn from the way they move, how they hit, and how they move their feet.

You can also learn how to score if you follow along.

scoring

The scoring is different: love, 15, 30, 40. If both players reach 40 points it is called "deuce", then the next point is "advantage", and finally, "game".

play

The best way to learn the game of tennis is to play it. Play a lot, and soon you will get better and better!